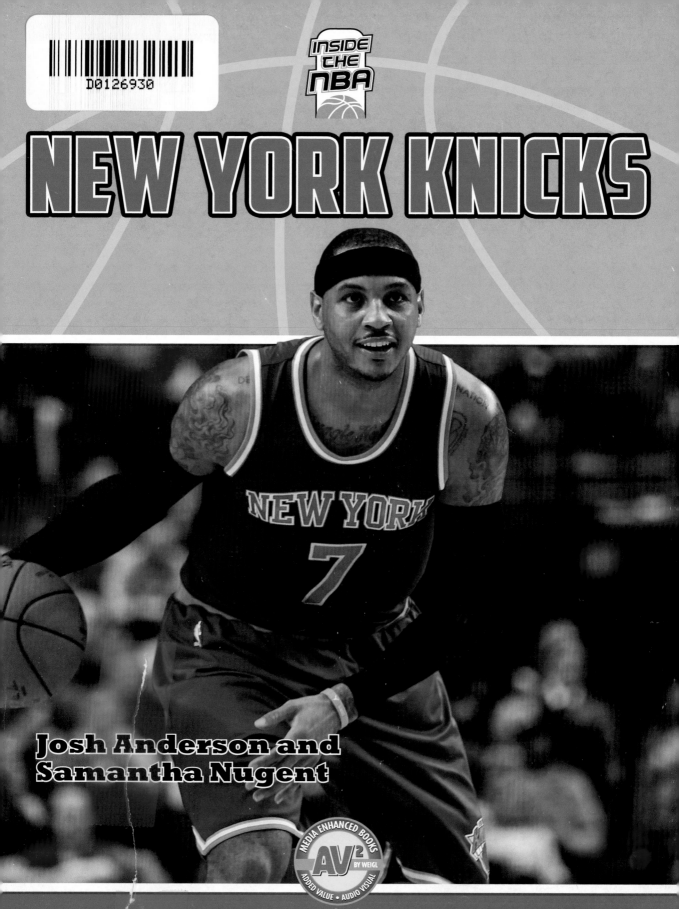

INSIDE THE NBA

NEW YORK KNICKS

Josh Anderson and Samantha Nugent

AV² provides enriched content that supplements and complements this book. Weigl's AV² books strive to create inspired learning and engage young minds in a total learning experience.

Your AV² Media Enhanced books come alive with...

Audio
Listen to sections of the book read aloud.

Key Words
Study vocabulary, and complete a matching word activity.

Video
Watch informative video clips.

Quizzes
Test your knowledge.

Go to **www.av2books.com**, and enter this book's unique code.

BOOK CODE

P 3 3 5 8 5 6

Embedded Weblinks
Gain additional information for research.

Slide Show
View images and captions, and prepare a presentation.

AV² by Weigl brings you media enhanced books that support active learning.

Try This!
Complete activities and hands-on experiments.

... and much, much more!

Published by AV² by Weigl
350 5th Avenue, 59th Floor
New York, NY 10118
Website: www.av2books.com

Library of Congress Control Number: 2016935111

ISBN 978-1-4896-4709-2 (Hardcover)
ISBN 978-1-4896-4710-8 (Multi-user eBook)

Printed in the United States of America in Brainerd, Minnesota
1 2 3 4 5 6 7 8 9 0 20 19 18 17 16

082016
200516

Project Coordinator Heather Kissock
Art Director Terry Paulhus

Photo Credits
Every reasonable effort has been made to trace ownership and to obtain permission to reprint copyright material. The publishers would be pleased to have any errors or omissions brought to their attention so that they may be corrected in subsequent printings.

Weigl acknowledges Newscom, Corbis Images, and Alamy as its primary image suppliers for this title.

CONTENTS

Introduction

Coming into the 2010–11 season, the New York Knicks had missed out on the National Basketball Association (NBA) **playoffs** for six straight seasons. As the 2010–11 season approached, the team started to remake its roster, acquiring talented players such as Raymond Felton and Amar'e Stoudamire. During the season, the team acquired nine-time **All-Star** Carmelo Anthony. Fans hoped these new additions would make the team a championship contender. By the end of the season, the Knicks had earned a spot in the postseason. The team went to the playoffs the next two seasons, too. Anthony led the league in scoring during the 2012–13 season, averaging 28.7 points.

Center Robin Lopez came to New York in 2015. In his first game with the Knicks, he posted 8 points.

After advancing to the Eastern **Conference** Semifinals in 2013, the Knicks missed the playoffs the next two years. The Knicks added a combination of young players and veterans before the 2015–16 season. The team now hopes players such as Robin Lopez, Aaron Afflalo, and Kristaps Porzing will bring renewed energy to the court as Anthony and the Knicks try to return to the postseason.

 Even before point guard Jose Calderon came to New York, he was considered one of the best free throw shooters in the league.

NEW YORK KNICKS

Arena Madison Square Garden

Division Atlantic Division (Eastern Conference)

Head Coach Jeff Hornacek

Location New York, New York

NBA Championships 2 (1970, 1973)

8 Conference Titles

9 Retired numbers

17 Hall of Famers

93 All-Star Selections

186 Playoff victories

History

The Knicks had their highest win percentage of

.732

during the 1969–70 season.

Forward Derrick Williams was traded to the New York Knicks in 2015. He puts up an average of nine points per game for the team.

The history of the New York Knicks dates back to the first game played in NBA history. The league was called the Basketball Association of America (BAA), and the team was called the Knickerbockers. The league's first game in 1946 matched the Knickerbockers against the Toronto Huskies. The Knickerbockers won 68–66, earning the first victory in the history of the league. The team's early years were mostly successful, but it did not earn its first NBA Championship until 1970.

The Knicks built themselves into playoff contenders in the late 1960s. The team was led by two of the league's best players, Walt Frazier and Willis Reed. In addition to winning its first title in 1970, the team won another in 1973. Both times, the Knicks defeated the Los Angeles Lakers in the **NBA Finals**.

From 1985 to 2000, the Knicks were home to one of the most successful players in NBA history. Patrick Ewing led the team to the playoffs every year from 1988 to 2000. He also led the Knicks to the Finals in both 1994 and 1999, where they narrowly missed out on winning the title. Since Ewing's departure in 2000, the Knicks have been to the postseason only five times. Recently, Kristaps Porzingis's strong rookie season in 2015–16 has given fans hope that the next great era of Knicks basketball is coming soon.

Knicks legend Dave DeBusschere has been named one of the 50 greatest players in NBA history. In 1983, he was inducted into the Basketball Hall of Fame.

The Arena

Madison Square Garden is home to the New York Knicks, the New York Islanders of the National Hockey League (NHL), concerts, boxing matches, and many other popular events.

The original Madison Square Garden opened in 1879 and could seat **10,000 guests**.

The Knicks home arena, Madison Square Garden, is nicknamed "The World's Most Famous Arena." While the Knicks have always called "the Garden" their home, the building has existed in several different locations. The Knicks first played in the third Madison Square Garden, located uptown from the current arena, in 1946. The historic building hosted many famous events, including President John F. Kennedy's birthday party in 1962.

The Knicks moved into the current location of the Garden in 1968 and have played there ever since. The 19,800-seat building is the second-oldest home arena in the NBA. From 1993 to 2002, the Knicks experienced a streak of 433 home sellouts, one of the longest in league history.

Nearly 40 million fans have attended Knicks home games since the team began playing in the league. The Garden's court design includes the Knicks' **logo** at center court, which is an orange basketball with the team name on top. The perimeter of the court and the free throw lanes are blue.

Part of Madison Square Garden's massive 2011–12 renovations included the installation of a huge LED scoreboard.

Where They Play

British Columbia

Alberta

Ontario

Saskatchewan

Manitoba

CAN.

Washington

Montana

North Dakota

Minnesota

Ontario

9
Oregon

Idaho

South Dakota

Wisconsin

7

25

5

10

Wyoming

Nevada

Utah

Nebraska

Iowa

21

Illinois

UNITED STATES

California

1

2

Colorado

6

Kansas

Missouri

8

Oklahoma

13

3

Arizona

New Mexico

Arkansas

4

11

Pacific Ocean

MEXICO

Texas

Louisiana

Miss

15

12

Gulf of Mexico

NBA WESTERN CONFERENCE

PACIFIC DIVISION
1. Golden State Warriors
2. Los Angeles Clippers
3. Los Angeles Lakers
4. Phoenix Suns
5. Sacramento Kings

NORTHWEST DIVISION
6. Denver Nuggets
7. Minnesota Timberwolves
8. Oklahoma City Thunder
9. Portland Trail Blazers
10. Utah Jazz

SOUTHWEST DIVISION
11. Dallas Mavericks
12. Houston Rockets
13. Memphis Grizzlies
14. New Orleans Pelicans
15. San Antonio Spurs

Newfoundland

Quebec

Prince Edward Island

New Brunswick

New Hampshire

Vermont

Madison Square Garden, New York

Maine

Nova Scotia

Massachusetts

Rhode Island

Connecticut

New York

New Jersey

Pennsylvania

Delaware

Maryland

District of Columbia

West Virginia

Virginia

Michigan

Ohio

Indiana

Kentucky

Tennessee

North Carolina

South Carolina

Alabama

Georgia

Florida

ADA

CANADA

ssippi

Atlantic Ocean

N W E S

30 · 23 · 22 · 28 · 26 · 27 · 29 · 20 · 24 · 17 · 16 · 14 · 19 · 18

MADISON SQUARE GARDEN™

Arena
Madison Square Garden

Location
4 Pennsylvania Plaza
New York, New York 10001

Broke Ground
1964

Completed
1967

Features
- Theater-style lighting
- Pennsylvania Station located beneath arena
- GardenVision scoreboard features 18 high-definition LED screens

LEGEND
☆ Madison Square Garden
⬛ Western Conference
⬛ Eastern Conference

NBA EASTERN CONFERENCE

SOUTHEAST DIVISION
16. Atlanta Hawks
17. Charlotte Hornets
18. Miami Heat
19. Orlando Magic
20. Washington Wizards

CENTRAL DIVISION
21. Chicago Bulls
22. Cleveland Cavaliers
23. Detroit Pistons
24. Indiana Pacers
25. Milwaukee Bucks

ATLANTIC DIVISION
26. Boston Celtics
27. Brooklyn Nets
★ 28. New York Knicks
29. Philadelphia 76ers
30. Toronto Raptors

The Uniforms

Several times during the 2015–16 season, the Knicks wore a **throwback alternate uniform** from the 1950s.

The Knicks uniforms of today are a throwback to the Championship Era uniforms of the 1970s.

The Knicks are one of the oldest **franchises** in the NBA. Their uniforms have remained consistent through the years. The team has almost always worn white uniforms at home and blue uniforms to away games, both with the words "New York" written across the chest. Over the years, various combinations of white, orange, and blue lettering have been used on the team's jerseys.

HOME

AWAY

The team's current home uniform is all white, with orange numbers and letters. Each player's jersey has his name written across the back in blue. The shorts have a blue waistband. The away uniforms are blue with "New York" across the front and each player's number written in orange. The players names on the back are white. The shorts have an orange waistband. Recently, the team has also introduced some alternate jerseys. On Christmas Day, the Knicks have worn orange jerseys. During an event honoring Latino heritage, the Knicks wore jerseys with "Nueva York" written across the front.

In 2013, the Knicks introduced their orange alternate uniform. It is the opposite of the blue uniform, using orange as the main color with blue trim.

The Coaches

As a player, Jeff Hornacek was an **NBA All-Star** in 1992.

Jeff Hornacek is the 28th head coach of the New York Knicks.

Walt Frazier

Walt Frazier was the team's point guard during both of the Knicks' NBA Championship seasons. His 14,617 points are the second-most in team history, and his 4,791 **assists** are a team record. In addition to his offensive prowess, Frazier was a tough defender. He was named to the NBA's All-Defensive team seven times. The seven-time All-Star was inducted into the Basketball Hall of Fame in 1987. Frazier remains an iconic member of the Knicks organization. Since 1989, Frazier has been the broadcast voice of the Knicks on radio and television, where he is known for his unique and colorful style of calling a game.

Position: Point Guard
NBA Seasons: 13 (1967–1980)
Born: March 29, 1945, Atlanta, Georgia

Carmelo Anthony

After leading Syracuse University to the National Collegiate Athletic Association (NCAA) Championship, Carmelo Anthony was selected in the **NBA Draft** by the Denver Nuggets. After playing in Denver for seven-and-a-half seasons, he joined the Knicks. Since coming to New York, Anthony has averaged more than 25 points and 7 rebounds per game. On January 24, 2014, Anthony broke Bernard King's franchise single-game scoring record in a victorious match against the Charlotte Bobcats by scoring 62 points. Anthony is a three-time United States Olympian and two-time gold medalist.

Position: Small Forward
NBA Seasons: 14 (2003–present)
Born: May 29, 1984, New York City, New York

The Greatest of All Time

There are several standout players on the Knicks roster who have worked hard to push the team to success. Often, there is one player who has become known as the "Greatest of All Time," or GOAT. This player has gone above and beyond to achieve greatness and to help his team shine.

Patrick Ewing

Position: Center • **NBA Seasons:** 17 (1985–2002)
Born: August 5, 1962, Kingston, Jamaica

Patrick Ewing was one of the most intimidating players in the NBA from the moment he stepped onto the court for the Knicks. He won the Naismith College Player of the Year Award during his senior season at Georgetown University in Washington, D.C. That same year, the Knicks picked Ewing first in the 1985 NBA Draft. The 11-time All-Star led the Knicks to the playoffs 13 times and to the NBA Finals twice.

Ewing holds the Knicks' all-time record in many statistical categories, including points, with 23,665, rebounds, at 10,759, and **blocks**, with 2,758. During the "Ewing Years," the Knicks were frequently one of the best defensive teams in the NBA. The team ranked in the top 10 for fewest points allowed during Ewing's illustrious Knicks career.

In the 1985–86 season, his first with the Knicks, Ewing won Rookie of the Year.

The New York Knicks retired Patrick Ewing's jersey number, 33, in 2003.

fun facts

#1 Ewing scored a career high 51 points in one game, on March 24, 1990.

#2 He started in 82 games in 3 seasons with the Knicks.

#3 Ewing finished eight seasons as a top-10 scorer.

#4 During the NBA Playoffs, Ewing scored 2,787 points for the Knicks.

Ewing was inducted into the Basketball Hall of Fame in 2008.

The Moment

John Starks' last-minute shot in game 2 of the 1993 Eastern Conference Finals is one of the most famous moments in Knicks history. It is simply called "The Dunk."

From 1991 to 1996, the Knicks and the Chicago Bulls matched up five different times in the postseason. While the Knicks were a strong defensive team, the Bulls had one of the greatest players of his generation, Michael Jordan. The Bulls eliminated the Knicks from the playoffs in four of those five years.

One of the legendary matchups between the Knicks and the Bulls occurred in 1993. In the second game of the playoffs, the Knicks led by three, with less than a minute remaining. A basket for the Knicks would secure the win.

New York's exciting guard, John Starks, dribbled the ball over half court. He spotted an opening and quickly drove toward the hoop. Before he could try to score, the Bulls' forwards, Horace Grant and Michael Jordan, leapt toward the rim. Starks jumped to the hoop, rising above his opponents, and slammed the ball through the rim. This is remembered as one of the greatest dunks in NBA history. The Knicks won the game, 96–91.

🏀 Thanks to the electrifying performances of star players, such as Patrick Ewing and Michael Jordan, the 1993 NBA playoffs have been called the greatest postseason in basketball history.

🏀 Patrick Ewing had 10 steals during the series against the Chicago Bulls. His defense was a big part of the Knicks' success.

All-Time Records

23 Most Career Triple-Doubles
Of the 83 **triple-doubles** in Knicks history, Walt Frazier has 23 of them.

45%

982 Most Career Three-Point Field Goals
John Starks made 982 three-point **field goals** as a member of the Knicks.

9

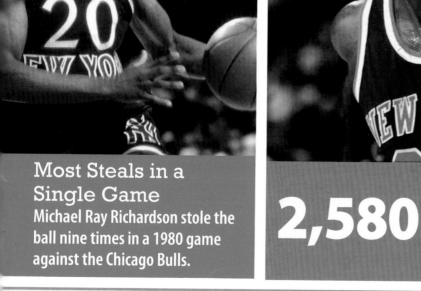

Highest Career Three-Point Percentage
In four seasons with the Knicks, Hubert Davis connected on nearly 45 percent of his three-point attempts.

22

Most Assists in a Single Game
Chris Duhon had 22 assists against the Golden State Warriors on November 29, 2008.

Most Steals in a Single Game
Michael Ray Richardson stole the ball nine times in a 1980 game against the Chicago Bulls.

2,580

Most Career Offensive Rebounds
From 1988 to 1998, Charles Oakley made 2,580 offensive rebounds as a member of the Knicks.

Timeline

Throughout the team's history, the Knicks have had many memorable events that have become defining moments for the team and its fans.

1970

The Knicks defeat the Los Angeles Lakers, 113–99, in game 7 of the NBA Finals. Walt Frazier leads the Knicks to the Championship with 36 points and 19 assists.

1946

New York is one of 11 cities granted a charter franchise in the Basketball Association of America.

 1950   **1960**   **1970**   **1980**

1973

The Knicks become the first team to ever defeat the Boston Celtics in game 7 of a playoff series. The 94–78 victory sends the Knicks back to the NBA Finals for a rematch with the Los Angeles Lakers.

1973

The Knicks defeat the Lakers, 102–93, in game 5 of the NBA Finals. Earl Monroe scores 23 points, and Willis Reed earns the NBA Finals Most Valuable Player Award for the second time.

19[85]

The first NBA D[raft Lottery] is held, and th[e Knicks win] the right to ch[oose first in] the upcoming N[BA Draft.] This leads the way [for the] team to select Georgeto[wn] center Patrick Ewing.

1999

The Knicks face off with the San Antonio Spurs in game 1 of the NBA Finals. The Spurs prevail, 89–77, over the Knicks, who are the only eighth-seeded team ever to advance to the NBA Finals.

1994

Patrick Ewing scores the key basket with 26.9 seconds left in the game, leading the Knicks to defeat the Indiana Pacers, 94–90, in game 7 of the Eastern Conference Finals. They earn their first trip to the NBA Finals in 21 seasons.

 1990   2000   2010   2020

1993

In a victory over the Lakers at Madison Square Garden, Ewing scores his 14,618th point, becoming the Knicks' all-time scoring leader.

The Future

The Knicks may have unearthed a star in the 2015 NBA Draft by selecting Kristaps Porzingis. With Porzingis and Anthony in place, the Knicks can compete for a spot in the NBA Playoffs. With some experience, and the development of young players such as Jerian Grant and Derrick Williams, championship contention may not be far off.

2013

The Knicks finish the season as Atlantic Division Champions for the first time since 1994. They advance to the Eastern Conference Semifinals.

Write a **[Biography]**

Life Story

A person's life story can be the subject of a book. T[his is ca]lled a biography. Biographies often descri[b]e the liv[es of people who have a]chieved great success. These people may be [al]ive to[day or they may have l]ived many years ago. Reading a biography can [help you learn] [a]bout a great person.

Get the Facts

Use this book, and research in the library and on the internet, to find out more about your favorite star. Learn as much about this player as you can. What position does he play? What are his statistics in important categories? Has he set any records? Also, be sure to write down key events in the person's life. What was his childhood like? What has he accomplished off the court? Is there anything else that makes this person special or unusual?

Use the Concept Web

A concept web is a useful research tool. Read the questions in the concept web on the following page. Answer the questions in your notebook. Your answers will help you write a biography.

Concept Web

Adulthood
- Where does this individual currently reside?
- Does he or she have a family?

Your Opinion
- What did you learn from the books you read in your research?
- Would you suggest these books to others?
- Was anything missing from these books?

Accomplishments off the Court
- What is this person's life's work?
- Has he or she received awards or recognition for accomplishments?
- How have this person's accomplishments served others?

Write a Biography

Childhood
- Where and when was this person born?
- Describe his or her parents, siblings, and friends.
- Did this person grow up in unusual circumstances?

Help and Obstacles
- Did this individual have a positive attitude?
- Did he or she receive help from others?
- Did this person have a mentor?
- Did this person face any hardships?
- If so, how were the hardships overcome?

Accomplishments on the Court
- What records does this person hold?
- What key games and plays have defined his career?
- What are his stats in categories important to his position?

Work and Preparation
- What was this person's education?
- What was his or her work experience?
- How does this person work?
- What is the process he or she uses?

Trivia Time

Take this quiz to test your knowledge of the New York Knicks.
The answers are printed upside down under each question.

1 What is the name of the Knicks' home arena?

A. Madison Square Garden

2 What position does Carmelo Anthony play on the court?

A. Small forward

3 In what year did the Knicks win their first NBA Championship?

A. 1970

4 Who holds the franchise record for most points scored?

A. Patrick Ewing

5 Who coached the Knicks to both of their NBA Championships?

A. Red Holzman

6 In what division do the Knicks play?

A. Atlantic Division

7 Who holds the franchise record for most assists in a single game?

A. Walt Frazier

8 Which player completed "The Dunk" against the Chicago Bulls in 1993?

A. John Starks

9 Which Knicks player led the league in scoring in 2012–13?

A. Carmelo Anthony

10 What team did the Knicks play against in the first game in NBA history?

A. Toronto Huskies

11 Who coached the Knicks to the NBA Finals in 1994?

A. Pat Riley

12 What team did the Knicks defeat in the 1973 NBA Finals?

A. Los Angeles Lakers

Key Words

All-Star: a mid-season game made up of the best-ranked players in the NBA. A player can be named an All-Star and then be sent to play in this game.

assists: a statistic that is attributed to up to two players of the scoring team who shoot, pass, or deflect the ball toward the scoring teammate

blocks: when a defensive player taps an offensive player's shot out of the air and stops it from getting to the basket

conference: an association of sports teams that play each other

field goals: baskets scored while the clock is running and the ball is in play

franchises: teams that are a member of a professional sports league

logo: a symbol that stands for a team or organization

NBA Draft: the annual event in June where NBA teams select players from college to join the league

NBA Finals: the last round of the NBA Playoffs, where one team from the Western Conference plays another team from the Eastern Conference and the winner is crowned NBA Champion

playoffs: a series of games that occur after regular season play

rebounds: taking possession of the ball after missed shots

triple-doubles: when a player accumulates a double digit number total in three of five statistical categories in a game. The categories are points, rebounds, assists, steals, and blocked shots.

Index

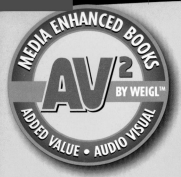

Log on to www.av2books.com

AV² by Weigl brings you media enhanced books that support active learning. Go to www.av2books.com, and enter the special code found on page 2 of this book. You will gain access to enriched and enhanced content that supplements and complements this book. Content includes video, audio, weblinks, quizzes, a slide show, and activities.

AV² Online Navigation

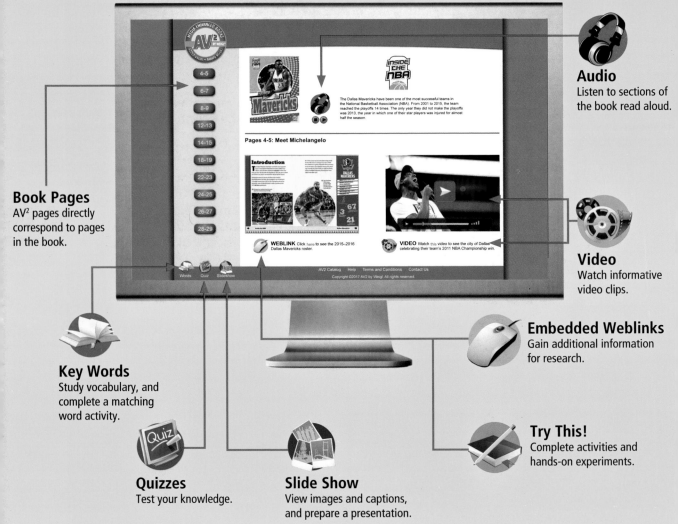

Audio
Listen to sections of the book read aloud.

Book Pages
AV² pages directly correspond to pages in the book.

Video
Watch informative video clips.

Key Words
Study vocabulary, and complete a matching word activity.

Embedded Weblinks
Gain additional information for research.

Quizzes
Test your knowledge.

Slide Show
View images and captions, and prepare a presentation.

Try This!
Complete activities and hands-on experiments.

AV² was built to bridge the gap between print and digital. We encourage you to tell us what you like and what you want to see in the future.

Sign up to be an AV² Ambassador at www.av2books.com/ambassador.